Gun Education and Safety

GUN RIGHTS & RESPONSIBILITIES

BRIAN KEVIN
ABDO Publishing Company

visit us at
www.abdopublishing.com

Published by ABDO Publishing Company, PO Box 398166, Minneapolis, MN 55439. Copyright © 2012 by Abdo Consulting Group, Inc. International copyrights reserved in all countries. No part of this book may be reproduced in any form without written permission from the publisher. The Checkerboard Library™ is a trademark and logo of ABDO Publishing Company.

Printed in the United States of America, North Mankato, Minnesota.
112011
012012

 PRINTED ON RECYCLED PAPER

Cover Photo: Corbis
Interior Photos: AP Images pp. 8, 9, 12, 15, 20, 21, 22–23, 27; Corbis pp. 6, 17, 18–19; Getty Images pp. 13, 28; Glow Images p. 4; iStockphoto p. 29; Neil Klinepier p. 24; National Archives and Records Administration p. 7; Thinkstock p. 5; US Marine Corps p. 11

Series Coordinator: Megan M. Gunderson
Editors: Megan M. Gunderson, BreAnn Rumsch
Art Direction: Neil Klinepier

Library of Congress Cataloging-in-Publication Data

Kevin, Brian, 1980-
 Gun rights & responsibilities / Brian Kevin.
    p. cm. -- (Gun education and safety)
 Includes index.
 ISBN 978-1-61783-315-1
 1. Firearms--Law and legislation--United States--Juvenile literature. 2. Gun control--United States--Juvenile literature. I. Title. II. Title: Gun rights and responsibilities.
 KF3941.K48 2012
 344.7305'33--dc23
                                    2011031412

CONTENTS

The Petition 4
The Second Amendment 6
The National Firearms Act 8
The Gun Control Act of 1968. 10
The Brady Law 12
Court Cases 14
World Rights 16
Concealed and Open Carry Laws 20
State Rights. 22
Gun Debates 26
Glossary 30
Web Sites 31
Index. 32

The Petition

One afternoon, Jamal answered the door to find a man with a clipboard standing on the porch. The man asked Jamal if his parents were home. When Jamal's mom came to the door, Jamal listened.

The man wanted her to sign a paper that was on the clipboard. But she didn't want to. The two talked and shook hands, and then Jamal's mom closed the door.

"What was that on the clipboard?" Jamal asked. His mom explained that the man was asking people to sign a petition. It was a way for people to show support for an idea.

This petition supported an open-carry law. The law would let people openly carry guns in public. Jamal knew his mom kept a pistol in a locked drawer. "Why didn't you sign it?" he asked.

Petitions are one way to show support for a cause. It's up to you to decide whether to sign.

"My gun is for protecting our home," Jamal's mom said. "I don't think it's safe to carry guns on the streets."

Jamal wondered if his mom had made the man angry. But she said that everyone feels differently about gun laws. "Guns come with rights and responsibilities," she told Jamal. "Part of that is always respecting the opinions of others."

The Second Amendment

Guns have been important in the United States since the country was founded. When the **American Revolution** started, the colonies had no army. Instead, each used a **militia**.

For the war, an army formed with George Washington in command. But afterward, many **Founding Fathers** wanted to return to a militia system.

In England, laws had allowed rulers to take guns away from people. Many Founding Fathers wanted to prevent this in their new country. They believed free men should have the right to keep and bear their own firearms.

The US **Constitution** went into effect in 1788. Ten amendments called the Bill of Rights came three years later. In them, the **Founding Fathers** created protection for gun rights.

The Second Amendment says, "A well regulated **Militia**, being necessary to the security of a free State, the right of the people to keep and bear Arms, shall not be infringed." That's a long sentence! And in more than 220 years, it has been interpreted in many ways.

The Bill of Rights

The National Firearms Act

By 1934, guns had changed a lot. Gone were the long, single-shot muskets of the **American Revolution**. Instead, machine guns and short-barrel shotguns were making headlines.

The Saint Valentine's Day Massacre of 1929 had helped give such guns a bad name. In Chicago, four gangsters had used them to kill seven rivals.

The Saint Valentine's Day killers worked for the famous gangster Al Capone.

As a result, Congress wanted to stop the sale of these guns. So in 1934, lawmakers passed the National Firearms Act (NFA). But this law didn't ban the guns. Instead, it placed a tax on their purchase.

The sawed-off shotgun is easy to hide. So, it became known as a criminal weapon.

Guns for hunting, target shooting, or personal protection were not taxed. But machine guns, sawed-off shotguns, **silencers**, and other weapons were.

The NFA tax added an extra $200 to the price of these guns. At the time, $200 was a lot of money! The tax hasn't changed since 1934. So these days, it doesn't actually prevent many sales. Still, the NFA has changed in other ways.

The Gun Control Act of 1968

When the NFA was passed, it stated owners must register certain types of guns. That way, the government could keep track of dangerous guns. Soon, this process caused problems.

In 1965, Miles Edward Haynes of Texas owned a sawed-off shotgun. But he never registered it. So, he was arrested and found guilty.

Haynes felt he had been in a tough position. If he had followed the NFA rule, he would have been admitting to owning an illegal firearm.

The Fifth Amendment in the Bill of Rights says citizens can't be forced to **incriminate** themselves. Haynes argued that the NFA did just that. The US **Supreme Court** agreed and withdrew his conviction in 1968.

The NFA needed some changes. So that year, Congress passed the Gun Control Act (GCA) of 1968. This act said gun owners didn't have to register guns they already owned. It also expanded the NFA to cover weapons such as grenades and bombs.

While Americans have the right to own guns, certain weapons require more control than others.

    The GCA said dealers could not sell guns to minors, **felons**, drug addicts, or the mentally ill. And, only certain dealers could sell guns across state lines.

    Some people said this law didn't solve enough problems. For example, a felon could still buy a gun with a fake name. Others believed that proved no law could really stop gun crime.

The Brady Law

Background checks began under the Brady Law in 1998.

About ten years later, the GCA didn't stop John Hinckley Jr. Hinckley had a police record and a history of mental illness. But in 1980, he used a fake address to buy a revolver.

Hinckley used the gun in an attempt to **assassinate** President Ronald Reagan on March 30, 1981. Luckily, he just wounded the president.

DETERMINED AND DEDICATED

James Brady *(left)* was badly wounded during Hinckley's attack on President Ronald Reagan. He was not able to continue in his work at the White House. However, he quickly turned his efforts toward gun laws.

In 1996, Brady received the Presidential Medal of Freedom. And in 2000, President Bill Clinton *(right)* named the White House Press Briefing Room after Brady. Today, Brady continues to support gun laws. He hopes they will protect both gun owners and non-gun owners.

However, Hinckley also wounded White House Press Secretary James Brady. Brady's injury left him partly **paralyzed**.

Many people felt that the shooting could have been prevented. They suggested requiring background checks for gun purchases. This would have kept Hinckley from buying the gun.

So Brady, his wife, and others worked to pass a new law. In 1993, President Bill Clinton signed the Brady Handgun Violence Prevention Act.

The Brady Law set up a criminal background check system. Anyone buying a gun from a federally licensed dealer must first pass this check. The law helps keep high-risk people from buying guns.

Court Cases

Gun laws are always changing. For example, recent laws have banned sales to anyone found guilty of **domestic abuse**. And, some semiautomatic guns are limited to use by police or military.

Over the years, court cases have helped make gun laws and rights more clear. In 1975, the District of Columbia banned handguns. Some people supported this ban. They believed the Second Amendment only protects guns for **militias**.

But, Dick Heller and five others thought the ban went against the Bill of Rights. So, they **sued** the District of Columbia.

The case reached the US **Supreme Court** in 2008. In *District of Columbia v. Heller*, the court ruled the Second Amendment protects guns for home defense. So, the District of Columbia had to once again allow handguns.

In 2010, the Supreme Court made a similar ruling in the *McDonald v. City of Chicago* case. The City of Chicago, Illinois, had also banned handguns. The court said this was **unconstitutional**. Both rulings helped solidify the range of the Second Amendment.

Over the years, Otis McDonald (below right) has faced increasing violent crime in his Chicago neighborhood. Soon after the Heller *decision, he began fighting for those who want to legally own a handgun for protection.*

World Rights

Thanks to the Second Amendment, Americans enjoy many gun rights. However, gun laws in other countries vary greatly.

In China, gun ownership is not protected by law. Most people are not allowed to own guns at all. Exceptions for hunting or protection from wildlife are rare.

Owning a gun illegally in China can be punished with two years in prison. And, selling a gun illegally can be punished by death.

The United Kingdom also has **strict** gun laws. Every gun purchase needs a license. And getting one is difficult.

Buying hunting rifles or handguns for target shooting means a long application process. The person applying must tell UK police why he or she wants a gun. Police talk with the person's doctor and other sources before approving the application.

Self-defense is a common reason for buying guns in the United States. That reason is not accepted in the United Kingdom.

The Swiss Army uses the SG-550 assault rifle. Soldiers may buy their own from the army after finishing their service.

Other countries have less tough gun laws. In Switzerland, most young men become members of the nation's **militia**. They are expected to keep their army rifles at home. Hunting weapons are available for other adults with the proper license.

In 2011, Swiss citizens voted on a firmer law some said would help prevent violent crime. But more people voted against the law. Some felt it would harm shooting clubs, which are an important part of many Swiss communities.

Gun laws have also become more relaxed in Saudi Arabia. Before 2009, Saudis could only buy hunting weapons from sporting goods stores. The government then decided to allow private gun stores.

A Saudi person must be 21 years old to buy a gun. But, he or she can begin learning to use one at age 12. An adult must be present.

It's easy to see how differently everyone feels about gun laws. In Finland, a 15-year-old can own a handgun with permission from a parent. But in Brazil, gun owners must be at least 25. And in South Africa, people can carry handguns in public without a permit. But in Australia, this is illegal.

Concealed and Open Carry Laws

Even within the United States, gun laws vary. One of the biggest issues relates to carrying guns in public. For example, can a gun owner take a gun to the mall? If so, should the gun be hidden? Or should it be allowed to hang from the owner's belt? Different people feel very strongly about carry laws.

Almost all states allow concealed carry. This means that gun owners can have hidden guns in public. In most cases, they need a permit from the state where they live.

Some states allow open carry, which means guns may be visible in public. This may or may not need a special permit. Sometimes, the same permit allows for either carry.

A few states ban open carry everywhere. Many ban it in specific places, such as college campuses.

People often discuss carry laws. Some think permits should never be required. Others say guns should never be allowed near schools.

In some states, businesses can ban guns on their property even if concealed carry is legal.

State Rights

As we have seen, gun laws change from state to state. So, a gun owner must learn the laws where he or she lives. When traveling to a different state, he or she also needs to know the gun laws there.

State laws also range in their level of gun control. California has **strict** gun laws. To buy a handgun, a buyer needs to get a permit and attend a safety class. There is a ten-day waiting period on all gun purchases. Open carry is not allowed, and concealed carry permits are hard to get.

In contrast, Arizona's gun laws are very relaxed. Owners can carry concealed guns without a permit. And, special training and practice are not needed. There are also no rules against carrying guns in cars.

Know and follow carry and permit laws! Ignoring them can lead to fines or jail time.

Other states fall somewhere in the middle. In New York, a concealed carry permit is available with police approval. Buying a handgun requires a license. But, there is no waiting period.

New Yorkers cannot travel in a car with a loaded rifle or shotgun. But with the proper license, handguns are permitted in cars.

Families in every state live with guns in their homes.

In Texas, people do not need a permit to buy a gun. Open carry is not allowed. However, concealed carry permits are easily available. Weapons in cars must be hidden.

The only state that bans all public carrying is Illinois. Illinois also requires waiting periods and licenses to buy guns.

No matter what state you live in, one thing doesn't change. Firearms owners are expected to be safe and respect others. The right to bear arms comes with the duty to know and follow the law.

How many people keep firearms in or around their homes?

0%-10% | 11%-20% | 21%-30%
31%-40% | 41%-50% | 51%-60% | 61%+

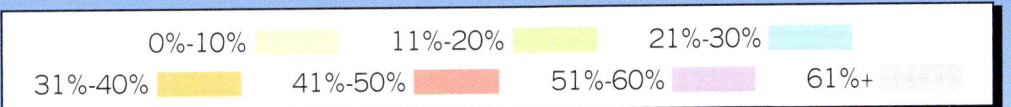

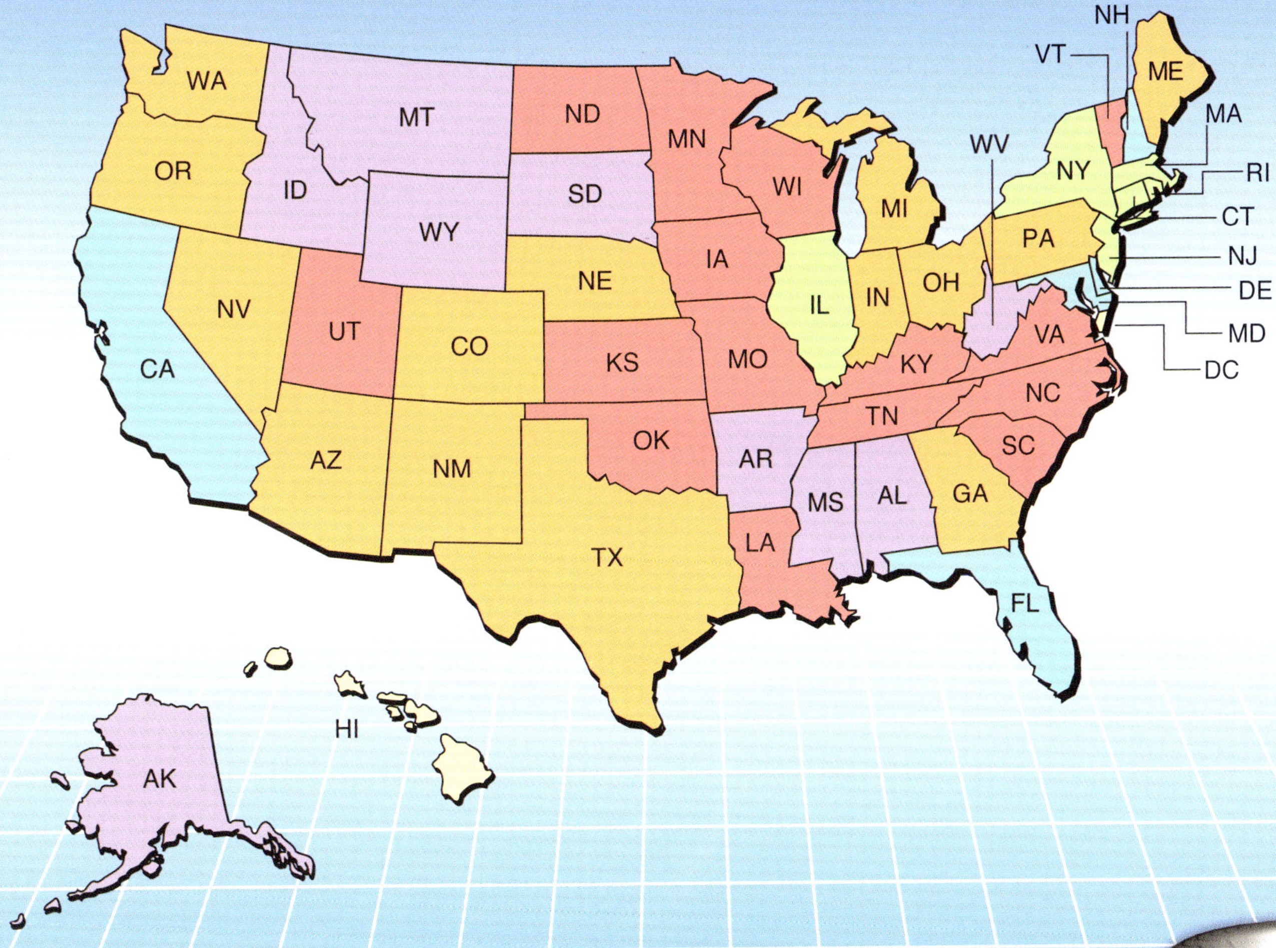

Gun Debates

You now know that some gun owners want fewer limits on their carry rights. Others may enjoy hunting but not approve of open carry. One non-gun owner may want to ban guns near schools. Yet another might support concealed carry.

It's important to talk with your local lawmakers about guns. This is true for those who own guns as well as those who do not.

After all, gun laws are always changing. For example, in 2010 Congress voted to allow people to carry loaded guns in national parks. Supporters say this will make people safer. Critics say the parks were never really that dangerous. They worry about risks to wildlife from careless gun owners.

There are many groups that support different views on guns. The well-known National Rifle Association (NRA) was founded in 1871 to encourage better shooting practices. It wasn't long before the NRA helped start hunter education. And, its members worked to pass gun-friendly laws.

The NRA and its supporters work for fewer limits on guns.

Today the NRA has nearly 4 million members. It still offers firearms education classes. Meanwhile, the NRA works with lawmakers who support gun rights. It also gives millions of dollars each year to this cause.

The Brady Center and the Brady Campaign both work for more limits on guns.

Unlike the NRA, the Brady Center to Prevent Gun Violence works to increase gun control. This group supports research and laws that prevent gun crimes. The Brady Center also helps fight court cases about gun rights.

The Brady Center supports tougher limits on who can own guns. One important focus is the "gun show loophole." Since 1993, background checks have been required to buy guns from licensed gun sellers, such as gun stores.

Whatever people's views about gun rights, everyone agrees that safety comes first.

However, unlicensed dealers can sell guns at gun shows. And, they don't have to perform background checks there. **Felons** and other high-risk people might buy guns this way. The Brady Center believes there should be a law to prevent this.

Groups such as the NRA and the Brady Center often disagree about gun laws. But all sides agree on the need for gun safety.

Preventing accidents and crime is important to everyone. Being smart with guns means knowing not only your rights but also your responsibilities!

GLOSSARY

American Revolution - from 1775 to 1783. A war for independence between Great Britain and its North American colonies. The colonists won and created the United States of America.

assassinate - to murder a very important person, usually for political reasons.

Constitution - the laws that govern the United States. Something that does not follow the Constitution is unconstitutional.

domestic abuse - violence between two adults who are in or have been in a close relationship, such as marriage.

felon - a person who has committed a felony, which is a serious crime.

Founding Fathers - members of the Constitutional Convention held in Philadelphia, Pennsylvania, in 1787. They helped establish the new US government.

incriminate - to accuse of a crime or show to be guilty.

militia (muh-LIH-shuh) - an army of citizens trained for emergencies and national defense.

paralyze - to cause a loss of motion or feeling in a part of the body.

silencer - a device that quiets the sound of a firearm.

strict - following or demanding others to follow rules or regulations in a rigid, exact manner.

sue - to bring legal action against a person or an organization.

Supreme Court - the highest, most powerful court in the United States.

To learn more about gun rights and responsibilities, visit ABDO Publishing Company online. Web sites about gun rights and responsibilities are featured on our Book Links page. These links are routinely monitored and updated to provide the most current information available.
www.abdopublishing.com

INDEX

B
background check 13, 28, 29
Bill of Rights 7, 10, 14
bomb 11
Brady, James 13
Brady Center to Prevent Gun Violence 28, 29
Brady Handgun Violence Prevention Act 13

C
Clinton, Bill 13
concealed carry 19, 20, 21, 22, 24, 26
Constitution, US 7, 14

F
Fifth Amendment 10

G
grenade 11
Gun Control Act of 1968 10, 11, 12
gun show 28, 29

H
Haynes, Miles Edward 10
Heller, Dick 14
Hinckley, John, Jr. 12, 13
history 6, 7, 8, 9, 10, 12, 13, 14, 26, 28
hunting 9, 16, 18, 19, 26

M
machine gun 8, 9
military 6, 7, 14, 18
musket 8

N
National Firearms Act 8, 9, 10
National Rifle Association 26, 27, 28, 29

O
open carry 4, 5, 19, 20, 21, 22, 24, 26

P
pistol 4, 5
police 14, 16, 24
protection 5, 9, 14, 16

R
Reagan, Ronald 12
revolver 12
rifle 16, 18, 24

S
Second Amendment 7, 14, 16
semiautomatic gun 14
shotgun 8, 9, 10, 24
silencer 9
Supreme Court, US 10, 14

T
target shooting 9, 16
tax 8, 9

W
waiting period 22, 24
Washington, George 6